I0023338

Benjamin D. Hill

Poems: devotional and occasional

Benjamin D. Hill

Poems: devotional and occasional

ISBN/EAN: 9783742860231

Manufactured in Europe, USA, Canada, Australia, Japa

Cover: Foto ©Thomas Meinert / pixelio.de

Manufactured and distributed by brebook publishing software
(www.brebook.com)

Benjamin D. Hill

Poems: devotional and occasional

POEMS:

DEVOTIONAL AND OCCASIONAL.

BY

BENJAMIN DIONYSIUS HILL, C.S.P.

———

NEW YORK:

THE CATHOLIC PUBLICATION SOCIETY,

9 WARREN STREET.

—

1877.

CONTENTS.

1

DEVOTIONAL: PART II.

MISCELLANEOUS.

OCCASIONAL.

4   CONTENTS.

BEATÆ :
SEMPER VIRGINI :
DEI GENITRICI :
MARIÆ.

PREFACE.

THE following poems, with one exception, have slowly accumulated during the past eight years. Several of them have appeared in the pages of the *Catholic World*. They are not arranged in chronological order, and the dates annexed to some of them are for private reasons. The "one exception" is the lyric called "Love's Prisoner," which was written in 1866, the year of the author's conversion to the faith.

The author has divided the Devotional poems into two Parts, in order to keep the First Part exclusively for Her at whose feet he lays the entire volume. The utterances of one of the greatest of her servants have furnished him a motto for this Part: and under such shelter he makes no apology for language which to

7

some may sound presumptuously familiar. All who can sympathize with the lines "To Be Forgiven" will not fail to understand him, he is sure.

If he shall have the happiness of making the Madonna something more than She has hitherto been to even one reader, he will not have failed wholly in his efforts for Her glory. But his chief aim is to inspire choice natures among young men in the world, and, still more, among his brethren in the Priesthood, with a *chivalrous* devotion to the Queen of queens.

When woman renounces earthly love "for the kingdom of heaven's sake," she finds in Our Lord the united love of Father, Brother, and Husband, and this in an Ideal Manhood she can never sufficiently adore and live for as her King. Have men, then, no corresponding Ideal when they elect for the "higher love"? Most assuredly they have—in Our Lady. They are free to find in Her the united love of Mother, Sister, and Spouse—united in an Ideal Womanhood they need not fear to worship too devoutly, or serve too

entirely, as their Queen. The Priest, especially,
as "Another Christ,"[1] both can and should find
in Mary all that She was to his Divine Model.

Now, let a man give his heart to the Immaculate—taking Her for the only Lady of his love,
serving Her and doing battle as Her "true
knight"—he will realize the *chivalrous* idea to
perfection. Those, moreover, who are acquainted
with the devotion taught by the Venerable Grignon De Montfort—whose writings have been
declared at Rome, in the process of his canoni-
zation, to contain "nothing contrary to faith or
morals, or *any new doctrine contrary to the
Church's common sentiment or practice*"[2]—will
recognize here, it is hoped, but a part of the
same devotion. And Father Faber says:[3] "I

---

[1] "Sacerdos Alter Christus."—S..Bernard.

[2] "Life and Select Writings of the Venerable Servant of
God, Louis-Marie Grignon De Montfort, etc." Translated from
the French. London: Thomas Richardson & Son; 1870. Preface, pp. xxvii., xxviii.

[3] In the preface (p. x.) to his translation of De Montfort's
"Treatise on the True Devotion to the Blessed Virgin."
Second Edition. London: Burns & Lambert; 1863.

cannot think of a higher work or a broader voca-
tion for any one than the simple spreading of
this peculiar devotion of the Venerable Grignon
De Montfort."

DEVOTIONAL.

PART I.

TO OUR BLESSED LADY.

"The Madonna should be our LOVE."
—St. Philip Neri.

1

TO A FAVORITE MADONNA.

LADY MARY, throne of grace,
 Imaged with thy Child before me:
Softly beams the perfect face,
 Fragrant breathes its pureness o'er me.

I but gaze, and all my soul
 Thrills as with a taste of heaven:
Passion owns the sweet control;
 Peace assures of sin forgiven.

Ah! then, what thy loveliness
 Where it shines divinely real,
If its strength has such excess,
 Feebly shadow'd in ideal!

In thine arms thy Royal Son
 Waits to fill us past our needing:
Hears for all, denied to none,
 Thy resistless whisper pleading.

Dream, say they, for poet's eye?
   Thou a dream! Then truth is seeming.
Only let me live and die
   Safely lost in such a dreaming!
1868.

HER NATIVITY.

Orietur Stella ex Jacob.—Num. xxiv. 17.

STAR of the Morning, how still was thy shining
   When its young splendor arose on the sea!
Only the Angels, the secret divining,
   Hailed the long-promised, the chosen, in thee.

Sad were the fallen, and vainly dissembled
   Fears of the Woman in Eden foretold:
Darkly they guessed, as believing they trembled,   .
   Who was the gem for the casket [1] of gold.

---

[1] " Thou art the casket where the jewel lay."—Geo. Herbert.

Oft as thy parents bent musingly o'er thee,
    Watching thy slumbers, and blessing their God ;
Little they dreamt of the glory before thee,
    Little thought *thee* Jesse's mystical Rod.[1]

Tho' the deep heart of the nations forsaken
    Beat with a sense of deliverance nigh ;
True to a hope, thro' the ages unshaken,
    Looked for the " day-spring " to break " from
        on high " ;

Thee they perceived not, the pledge of redemp-
    tion—
Hidden like thought, tho' no longer afar :
Not tho' the light of a peerless exemption
    Beamed in thy rising, Immaculate Star !

All in the twilight so modestly shining
    Dawned thy young beauty, sweet Star of the Sea !
· Only the Angels, the secret divining,
    Hailed the elected, " the Virgin," [2] in thee.

---

[1] Is. xi. 1.   [2] Is. vii. 14. ἡ Παρθένος.—LXX.

"SUPER OMNES SPECIOSA."[1]

Is any face that I have seen—
　Some perfect type of girlhood's face?
　Some nun's, soul-radiant, full of grace?—
Like thine, my beautiful, my Queen?

Of all the eyes have paused on mine—
　And these have met some wondrous eyes,
　So large and deep, so chaste and wise—
Have any faintly imaged thine?

The chisel with the brush has vied
　Till each seems victor in its turn;
　And love is ever quick to learn,
Nor throws the proffer'd page aside:

[1] Antiphon.

Yet few the glimpses it has caught:
   For thou transcendest all that art
   Can show thee—even to the heart
Most skill'd to read the poet's thought.

That thought can pierce its native sky
   Beyond the artist's starry guess:
   But all that it may dare express
Is thro' the worship of a sigh.

And this thou art, a sigh of love—
   Love that created as it sighed,
   And shaped thee forth a peerless bride
Dower'd for the spousals of the Dove.

To set the music of thy face
   To earthly measure, were to give
   Th' informing soul, and make it *live*
As there—God's uttermost of grace.

LILIUM INTER SPINAS.[1]

O FOUND at last—and *not* too late!
  O found, and never to be lost!
(Can death divide as at its gate?
    Change blight as with its frost?)

O found at last, forgive, forgive,
  This self-deceiving heart of mine,
That, knowing thee, it dared to live
    For other love than thine!

Eve's fairest daughters share her doom,
  Save thee, of sin, decay, and death:
Their beauty ripens for the tomb,
    Or fleets too soon for breath.

[1] Cant. ii. 2.

And some may prove, that guileless are,
    The sirens of a nether flood :
While thou dost lead us, like a star,
    Thro' pureness up to God.

O found at last—unhoped ideal !
    Thy poet's heart *must* live in thee :
Or gasp and wither for the· real,
    And roam a shoreless sea !

1868.

Sweet Name of Mary, name of names save
   One—
   And that, my Queen, so wedded unto thine
   Our hearts hear both in either, and enshrine
Instinctively the Mother with the Son—
The lisping child's new accent has begun,
   Heaven-taught, with thee: first fervent happy
     youth
   Makes thee the watchword of its maiden truth;
Repentant age the hope of the undone.
To me, known late but timely, thou hast been
   The noonday freshness of a wooded height;
   A vale of soothing waters; the delight
Of fadeless verdure in a desert scene.
And when, ere long, my day shall set serene,
   Be Hesper [1] to an eve without a night.

---

[1] The evening star.

Mother of God! My Queen is simply this.
 For this elected, the eternal Mind
Conceived her in its infinite abyss,
 With the God-Man co-type of human kind.
 And she, when came the wondrous hour assigned,
Conceiving her Conceiver, girt Him round,
 And held in her Immaculate womb confined
Whom "heav'n and the heav'ns of heav'ns cannot
 bound." [1]
Then brought Him forth, her little one, her own;
 And fed her suckling at her maiden breast—
 The only pillow of His earthly rest,
And still for evermore His dearest throne.
O Lady! what the worship Faith allows?
The Eternal calls thee Daughter, Mother, Spouse!

---

[1] Si cœlum, et cœli cœlorum capere eum nequeunt.—2 Paral.
ii. 6.

THE Mother of all mothers, yet no less
    The Virgin of all virgins! Yea, the more:
For 'tis from thy deific fruitfulness
    Have drawn all virgins their perennial store.
Since virgin Eve grew mother of our loss
    Virginity was barren—until thine,
Which bore the Fruit that in the press of the
    Cross
    Redeem'd us with the virgin-making wine.[1]
And now virginity may wed thy Son,
    Becoming thus the mother of fair deeds.
Still, after all the glories it has won
    In following the Lamb where'er He leads,
How peerless thine in having drawn Him down
And brought Him forth—the virgin's Spouse and
    Crown!

[1] Zach. ix. 17.

28

MOTHER of Christ—then Mother of us all.
   Mother of God made Man, of Man made
      God.[1]
The thornless garden, the immaculate sod,
Whence sprang the Adam that reversed the fall.
Mother of Christ, the Body mystical—
   Of us the members, as of Him the Head :
   Of Him our life, the first-born from the dead ;[2]
Of us baptized into His burial.[3]
Yes, Mother, we were truly born of thee
   On Calvary's second Eden—thou its Eve :
Thy dolors were our birth-pangs by the tree
   Whereon the second Adam died to live—
To live in us, thy promised seed to be,
   Who then his death-wound to the snake didst
      give.

---

[1] "Deus factus est homo, ut homo fieret Deus."—S. Augustino.

[2] Col. i. 18.   [3] Rom. vi. 4.

I.

SHE knelt, expectant, thro' the night,
  For IIe had promised. In her face
  The pure soul beaming, full of grace,
But sorrow-tranced—a frozen light.

But ere her eastward lattice caught
  The glimmer of tho breaking day,
  No more in Joseph's garden lay
The buried picture of her thought.

The seal'd stone shut a void, and lo—
  The Mother and tho Son had met!
  For her a day should never set
Had burst upon the night of woe.

24

In sudden glory stood He there,
  And gently raised her to His breast :
  And on His heart, in perfect rest,
She poured her own—a voiceless prayer.

Enough for her that He *has* died,
  And lives, to die again no more :
  The foe despoil'd, the combat o'er,
The Victor crowned and glorified.

II.

What song of Seraphim shall tell
  Thy joy to-day, my blissful Queen ?
  Yet truly not in vain, I ween,
Our earthly alleluias swell.

It is but just that we should thus
  Our Jesus' triumph share with thee.
  For *us* He died, to set us free :
Thou owest Him risen, then, to *us*.

But thou, sweet Mother, grant us more
   Than here to join the festive strain.
   To hymn, but never know, our gain,
Were ten times loss for once before.

Thy faithful children let us be.
   Entreat thy Son, that He may give
   The wisdom to our hearts to live
In His, the risen, life with thee.

For so, amid the onward years,
   This feast shall bring us strength renewed:
   To pass secure, o'er self subdued,
To Easter in the sinless spheres.

ORDINANDUS.

THE goal: and yet my heart is low,
  When rather should it brim with glee
They tell me this is ever so.
Ah well! I cling to one I know:
      Sweet Virgin, keep thou me.

O thou for whom I venture all—
  The fragile bark, the treacherous sea
(I needs must serve my Lady's call—
Her captive knight, her helpless thrall)—
      My pilot, keep thou me.

From tyranny of idle fears,
  And subtle frauds to make me flee—
Distorting unto eyes and ears
The burden of the coming years—
      My mercy, keep thou me.

From shirking the accepted cross,
  For all the galling that must be:
From seeing gold in what is dross,
And seeking gain in what is loss,
    My wisdom, keep thou me.

From lures too strong for flesh and blood—
  With show of ripe philosophy,
That points the fallen, who had stood
Contented with the lesser good—
    My victory, keep thou me.

O Lady dear, in weal, in woe,
  Till heaven reveal thy Son and thee,
Thy true love's mantle round me throw:
And tenderly, calmly, sweetly so,
    My glory, keep thou me.

1870.

ORDINATUS.

" Sicut lætantium omnium:
  habitatio est in Te."—Ps. lxxxv:

HEART of Mary, be my home
Thro' the toilsome years to come:
Few or many let them be,
So I live them all in thee.

Be my chapel when I pray:
Be my altar day by day:
Be my recollection sweet,
My perpetual retreat.

If thy priest (for such my trust)—
Keep me pure and mild and just:
Thy apostle—give me power:
If thy poet—be my bower.

1871.

DOMUS DOMINI DOMUS MEA.

"Lætatus sum in his, quæ dicta sunt mihi:
In Domum Domini ibimus."—Ps. cxxi.

How bold I grow in this new love,
  To ask thy Heart, that I may rest
Where thy Creator-Spouse, the Dove,
  Has made His dearest, sweetest nest:

Full wise I ask it. Have I turn'd
  Elsewhere, 'tis only not in vain
Because a lesson I have learn'd
  Which needs not to be taught again:

That other home is none for me.
  Tho' many a gentle heart might prove
An isle to touch at on the sea,
  My bark were portless should I rove.

Then let thy bosom b
And am I bold? 'l
Thy Son, my Brother,
And dwell with Hir

LAST

An, had I never lov'd
To thee my first, n
Tho' thou dost seem
My Dearest, my B

O darkness of the wa
When to invoke th
Was theme for school
For mine the loss—

I feel (unless too fon
That, had 1 known
Thy face had kept m
Since first it look'd

My eager soul "must needs have loved"
  So fair a "highest," had it "seen" : [1]
And time had made thee, as it moved,
  From boyhood's Mother manhood's Queen.

Yet can I murmur? Like thy Son,
  'Tis thine, O love, to glory more
In some frail, wounded, rescued *one*,
  Than nine-and-ninety safe before.

Thou hold'st me dearer for that past
  Where thou didst seek me at my worst:
And knowest that, if lov'd the last,
  My last is *best*—and best is first.

[1] " We needs must love the highest when we see it."—Tennyson.

I CALL thee "Love"—"my sweet, my dearest Love":
   Nor feel it bold, nor fear it a deceit.
Yet I forget not that, in realms above,
   The thrones of Seraphs are beneath thy feet.

If Queen of angels thou, of hearts no less:
   And so of mine—a poet's, which must needs
Adore to all melodious excess
   What cannot sate the rapture that it feeds.

And then thou art my Mother: God's, yet mine!
   Of mothers, as of virgins, first and best:
And I as tenderly, intimately thine
   As He, my Brother, carried at the breast.

My Mother! 'tis enough. If mine the right
   To call thee this, much more to muse and sigh
All other honeyed names. A slave, I might—
   A son, I must. And both of these am I.

33

KEEP me, sweet Love! Thy keeping is my rest.
  Not safer feels the eaglet from beneath
The wings that roof the inaccessible nest,
Than I when thou art near me, dearest, best—
  Whose love my life is, yea, my very breath!
  Thy Son to Egypt fled to prove our faith.
Not Herod's men had snatch'd Him from *thy*
        breast,
  Or changed His thronèd slumber into death.
How wonderful thy keeping, mighty Queen!
  So close, so tender: and as if thine eyes
Had only me to watch, thine arm to screen;
  And this inconstant heart were such a prize!
  And thou the while, in beatific skies,
Art reigning imperturbably serene!

34

SCAPULIS SUIS OBUMBRABIT TIBI.[1]

O LOVE, I pray thee guard my bed:
   And evermore, when I recline,
From thy sweet picture at its head
   There falls a pureness which is thine.

I feel thy shadow, and am blest:
   I know I shall not be defiled.
And oh, at times I seem to rest
   On thy own bosom—like a child!

If break my slumber, straight to thee
   My thought, in loving murmurs, flies—
As thou wert bending over me:
   And scarcely would thy face surprise.

[1] Ps. xc.—*Office of Compline.*

And should I die, what sweeter death?
  To dream my spirit out of night—
Thy whisper for the morning's breath,
  Thy smile to wake me into light!

UNDER A CLOUD.

MOTHER, it were death to doubt thee:
  Hell were Paradise to that!
Sooner would I stand without thee
  In the Vale of Josaphat! [1]

Ah, Belovèd, thou canst never
  See me wounded and defiled,
When thy pity's least endeavor
  Needs must save thy foolish child!

[1] It is commonly believed that the Last Judgment will be
held in this va'ley.

But for thee how vain my toiling !
   All is weakness—vileness all.
Tyrant self the gain despoiling :
   Fresh the trial, fresh the fall.

Give me, then, to feel thee near me
   When I tremble in eclipse :
Make me sure thou still dost hear me
   When the dry heart mocks the lips.

Love me, love me, dearest Mother !
   "Better is thy love than wine."
What to me were any other,
   If I knew I had not thine ?

"SPES AGONIZANTIUM."

Thou wilt come to me in death—
  Come and take me to thy Son?
Come before my fitful breath
  Passes and the strife is done?

When returning fears increase;
  When the past eclipses heaven;
Thou wilt come and whisper peace—
  Tell me it is all forgiven?

Thou wilt lend thy beauty's light
  When my darkness seeks thy face?
Beam, and let my failing sight
  Hail thee present "full of grace"?

When the swimming world is gone,
  When that other life is mine,
Thou wilt take me to thy Son?
  He will judge me but as thine?

38

Such my trust. O sweet my Love,
　Who has trusted thee and wept?
Choose one more, then—just to prove
　How thy promises are kept.

PER VINCULA LIBER.

LADY, my mercy! what the prize
　You saw in me I cannot think,
What time you "turn'd those pitying eyes"
　And snatch'd me from perdition's brink.

I call'd you not, that you should pray;
　Nor knew you: yet the grace was won.
You took, unask'd, your own sweet way
　To bring me captive to your Son.

And now in Him I live anew:
　With His dear gifts my soul is fair:
From His Heart comes its love of you,
　His breath the fragrance of its prayer.

Yet, Lady, tho' I dare not doubt
  ('Twere sin) your goodness or your power,
I dread, and more than foes without,
  This self—sure traitor every hour.

My peace that I must needs trust you,
  My safety that you trust not me.
Be tyrannous—to keep me true:
  Load me with chains—to make me free.

"*O VALDE DECORA!*"[1]

Could I but see thee, dear my Love!
  That face—but once! Not dazzling bright:
  Not as the blest above
    Behold it in God's light:

[1] Antiphon.

"O VALDE DECORA!"

But as it look'd at La Salette;
  Or when, in Pyrenean wild,
    It beamed on Bernadette,
      The favor'd peasant child.

Once seen—a moment—it would blind
  These eyes to beauty less than thine:
    And where could poet find
      Such theme for song as mine?

But if I ask what may not be,
  So spell me with thy pictur'd face,
    That haunting looks from thee
      May hold me like a grace.

Alone with Nature, in a round
　　Of beauty 'neath a cloudless blue,
To drink each spell of sight and sound,
　　For ever old, for ever new;

Or, dreaming with the dreaming lake,
　　That lovelier seems with every hour,
To muse the noon out, half-awake,
　　In shade of tent or leafy bower:

All this had been in other years
　　A joy as sweet and pure as now;
Had moved, perhaps, forgotten tears,
　　A fresher heart, a blither brow.

Yet base were I to wish it back—
　　That time the poet can recall
As Eden lost. The scene would lack
　　A dearer charm, the queen of all.

The lake would own no Lady then :
  Or if a mortal reign'd within,
What spoke of *her* would bid me ken
  The winter of the once hath been.

But now, O Love, 'tis *thou* art here—
  Within, and so without. To me
In Nature's glories thine appear:
  For God has made His world for Thee.

LAKE GEORGE, Aug., 1871.

NEVERMORE.

I WATCHED, from the lake, love's planet set
  Toward the mountain's ebon bar.
I said: "This hour the eyes are wet
  That bid adieu to *their* love's star.

"It rose so fair, and shone so bright,
  A twilight spell—how swiftly o'er!
For change the cloud, or death the night,
  That draws the murmur'd ' Nevermore ' ! "

But thou, thy poet's star of love,
   Madonna! if these eyes are wet,
That hail thee beautiful above,
   'Tis not that *thou* must pale and set.

'Tis joy that overflows in tears
   From out a heart at perfect rest:
With thee to rule my rescued years,
   O when was bard so deeply blest?

Ah, keep me true, my dearest Queen!
   That I may sing, as none before,
The sweetest love hath ever been,
   A star that setteth—nevermore.

LAKE GEORGE, Aug., 1871.

THE moon, behind her pilot-star,
    Came up in orbèd gold;
And slowly near'd a fleecy bar
    O'erfloating lone and cold.

I looked again and saw an isle
    Of amber on the blue:
So changed the cloudlet by the smile
    That softly lit it through.

Another look, the isle was gone—
    As tho' dissolved away.
And could it be so warmly shone
    That chaste and tender ray?

I said: "O star, the Faith art thou
    That brought my life its Queen—
In her sweet light no longer now
    The vapor it has been.

[1] Ps. xxxv. 10.

"Shine on, my Queen: and so possess
  My being to its core,
That self may shew from less to less,
  Thy love from more to more."

A touch of the oars, and on we slid—
  My cedar boat and I.
The dreaming water faintly chid
  Our rudeness with a sigh.

LAKE GEORGE, Sept., 1873.

Predestined second Eve. For this conceived
  Immaculate—not lower than the first.
  Chosen beginner in the loss reversed,
And mediatress in the gain achieved,
When, the new angel, as the old, believed,
  Thy hearkening should bless whom Eve's had
    curst.
  And therefore we, whose bondage thou hast
    burst,
Grateful for our inheritance retrieved,
Must deem this jewel in thy diadem
  The brightest: hailing thee alone " all fair "
  Nor ever soil'd with the original stain.
Alone, save Him whose Heart-blood bought the
    gem
  With peerless grace preventive none might
    share—
  Redemption's perfect end, all else tho' vain.

47

IMMACULATE! The very word
  Was made for thee, my blessed Love!
The one low note by angels heard,
  As o'er thee hung the brooding Dove,

In that still moment when thy soul
  Became its generate body's form;
And from the Cross to grace it stole
  A ruddy gleam Redemption-warm.

DECEMBER 8, 1875.

I.

"And didst thou die, dear Mother of our Life?
  Sin had no part in thee: then how should
    death?
Methinks, if aught the great tradition saith
Could wake in loving hearts a moment's strife"
(I said—my own with Her new image rife),
  "'Twere this." And yet 'tis certain, next to
    faith,
Thou didst lie down to render up thy breath;
Tho' after the Seventh Sword no meaner knife
Could pierce that bosom. No, nor did. No sting
  Of pain was there, but only joy. The love
    So long thy life ecstatic, and restrained
From setting free thy soul, now gave it wing:
  Thy body, soon to reign with it above,
    Radiant and fragrant, as in trance, remained.

49

II.

Yes, Mother of God, tho' thou didst stoop to
 die,
  Death could not mar thy beauty.   On thy
  face
  Nor time nor grief had wrinkle left or
  trace :
It had but aged in God-like majesty .
Mature, yet, save the mother in thine eye,
  As maiden-fresh as when, of all our race,
  Thou, first and last, wast greeted " full of
  grace "—
Ere thrice five years · had worshipt and gone
  by.
Mortal thy body : yet it could not know
  Mortality's decay. Like sinless Eve's,
   It waited but the change on Thabor
   shown.
And when, at thy sweet will, 'twas first laid
  low,
  Untainted as a lily's folded leaves
   It slept—the angels watching by the stone.

III.

"At thy sweet will." Then wherefore didst
    thou will
  To pass death's portal? To the outward ear
  There comes no answer; but the heart can
    hear.
Thy Son had past it. Thou upon "the hill
Of scorn" hadst stood beside the cross; wouldst
    still
  "Follow the Lamb where'er He went." Of fear
  Thou knewest naught. The cup's last drop, so
    dear
To Him, thy love must share—or miss its fill.
But more. Thy other children—even we—
  Must enter life thro' death. And couldst thou
    brook
  To watch our terrors at the dark unknown,
Powerless to stay us with a sympathy
  Better than any tender word or look—
    Bidding our steps tread firmly in thine
    own?

THE THREE EDENS.

"Ascende, Domine, in requiem tuam:
Tu et Arca sanctificationis tuæ."—Ps. cxxxi.

BLOOM'D the first Eden not with Man alone,
　　But Woman, equal Woman, at his side:
　　And seemly was it when, together tried,
They fell together—for the two were one.
On Calvary stood the Mother by the Son:
　　New Eve with second Adam crucified:
　　And as thro' Eve in Adam we had died,
Thro' Mary was our loss, in Christ, undone.
Then how should not the Paradise regained
　　Behold its Eve beside her Adam throned:
Both risen, both ascended—unprofaned
　　Each virginal body, by the grave disowned?
Else had our Foe his conquest half maintained:
　　The primal ruin been but half atoned.

FEAST OF THE ASSUMPTION, 1874.

'Tis round me with the air I breathe
　And o'er me like the heaven above,
And steadfast as the earth beneath—
　The mystery of Mary's love!

Chaste love—the truest, tenderest all
　Of mother, sister, spouse in one:
My strength in trial and in fall,
　My glory when the strife is done:

Chaste fire, consume my life away!
　Burn out this self, this sensual dross
That clings to pleasures of a day,
　And hankers for the gain of loss!

53

I.

Sole rest, of womankind, for hearts that crave
  Immaculate perfection! Only shrine
  For love that is religion—this of mine!
No Casta Diva Rome or Hellas gave
To school-boy years (so prone to dream and
      rave),
  No form ideal I was wont to pine
  At finding not, nor mortal deem'd divine,
Could sate my heart—which, hungry as the
    grave,
Made dust of all it gorged. I know not Thee.
  A barren creed had starved me. With the
    hour
  That brought me faith's realities, arose
The One mine eyes were purified to see :
  And wiser manhood built itself a bower—
  A temple of all-musical repose.

54

II.

' Who hast alone INVIOLATE remained," '
  Sings Holy Church. And I too, Lady sweet,
  Can find no word to murmur at thy feet
Melodious as this—which thou hast deigned
To hear so often from a love unfeigned.
  Ah, could my heart the melody repeat
  (Accept the wish, at least) at every beat,
And pour a ceaseless worship unrestrained !
Inviolate soul, inviolate body, thine.
  Sin could not touch thee, nor the tempter near :
  Pain no disease, and age no blemish gave :
More virgin for thy Motherhood Divine :
  Serene, sublime, 'mid sorrows without peer :
  Beauteous in death, untainted in the grave.

---

1 " Quæ sola inviolata permansisti."—Antiphon.

My Queen, thou knowest I would bring all
    hearts
  To love thee, if I could—and more than mine.
    Mine should be last and least. For love of
    thee,
    Unlike all other, breeds not jealousy,
  But rather makes its captive moan and pine
(Sure proof that 'tis a passion grace imparts)

To see thee lov'd thy due. But ah, if all
  Of Adam's race should love thee with the
    love
    Of Joseph and of John, 'twere not thy
    due!
    For this no more the many than the
    few
  Suffice, nor would yon myriad worlds above
Peopled with souls had never known a fall.

The gather'd love of Angels fails no less.
　'Tis God's alone can satisfy the claim—
　　And that (glad thought!) o'erflows the mea-
　　　sure's brim.
　Yet should I find deficiency in Him,
Did He not call thee by the dearest name
Of Mother, and with human lips express

A human Heart. But now I may not pine.
　The Heart of Jesus loves thee all thy due
　　(A love the sweeter that there is but one)..
　　And with His Heart *I* love thee, and atone
For hearts estranged, or lukewarm, or half-
　　true,　·
And all the base inconstancies of mine.

OCTOBER, 1876.

DEVOTIONAL.

***

PART II.

MISCELLANEOUS.

God an infant—born to-day!
  Born to live, to die, for me!
Bow, my soul: adoring say,
  "Lord, I live, I die, for Thee."
Humble then, but fearless, rise;
Seek the manger where He lies.

Tread with awe the solemn ground
  Tho' a stable mean and rude,
Wondering angels all around
  Throng the seeming solitude:
Swelling anthems, as on high,
Hail a second Trinity.[1]

'Neath the cavern's[2] dim-lit shade
  Meekly sleeps a tender form.

---

[1] Jesus, Mary, and Joseph are called the Earthly Trinity.
[2] It was a cavern used as a stable.

God on bed of straw is laid!
   Breaths of cattle keep Him warm !
King of glory, can it be
Thou art thus for love of me?

Hail, my Jesus, Lord of might!
   Here in tiny helpless band
Thy creation's infinite
   Holding like a grain of sand !
Hail, *my* Jesus—all my own:
Mine as if but mine alone!

Hail, my Lady, full of grace!
   Maiden-Mother, hail to thee !
Poring on the radiant face,
   Thine a voiceless ecstasy ;
Yet, sweet Mother, let me dare
Join the homage of thy prayer.

Mother of God—O wondrous name !
   Bending Seraphs hail thee Queen.

Mother of God, yet still the same
  Mary thou hast ever been:
Still so lowly, tho' so great—
Mortal, yet Immaculate!

Joseph, hail—of gentlest power!
  Shadow of the Father [1] thou:
Thine to shield in danger's hour
  Whom thy presence comforts now.
Mary trusts to thee her Child;
He His Mother undefiled.

Jesus, Mary, Joseph, hail!
  Saddest year its Christmas brings:
Comes the faith that cannot fail,
  Come the shepherds and the kings:
Gold and myrrh and incense sweet
Come to worship at your feet.

[1] See Faber's *Bethlehem*.

ON A PICTURE OF NAZARETH.

In dreams no longer, but reveal'd to sight,
  Comes o'er me, like a vision after death,
That shrine of tenderest worship, that delight
  Of loftiest contemplation—Nazareth.

Fair-throned as when creation's King and Queen
  Abode within its walls, it looks around
As scorning time and change; tho' these have
    been
  The ruthless masters of its hallow'd ground.

Still smiling as of old, it catches still
  As fresh a morning; basks in such a noon;
Hears evening's voice as sweetly softly thrill:
  In glory sleeps beneath a gushing moon.

Still looms the Mountain of Precipitation
  In sadness o'er a vale serene and bright;

As when the Saviour foil'd His frenzied nation,
  Who fain had cast Him headlong from the
    height.

And see upon the slope the very gate
  Where—spot to kiss!—Her lowly footstep fell,
As daily pass'd the Maid Immaculate
  To fill her pitcher yonder at the well.

That well! where mirror'd shone the loveliest
    face
  That ever woman wore! 'tis there—the same!
Tho' hating Christ and Juda's banish'd race,
  The Moslems honor there the Virgin's name.

Give thanks, my soul: give thanks that thou hast
    seen.
  Make Nazareth all a well of grace; and pray
To keep its taste within thee—which has been
  The strength of saints.   Drink deep: and go
    thy way.
    1870.

BETHLEHEM, House of Bread,[1]
   Of the Bread that came down from
      heaven.[2]
  "For the life of the world 'tis given:
Eat of it," Jesus said.

         •

  "Father," He bade us pray,
   "Give us this heavenly bread"
   ("Ours" we must call it, He said):
  "Give us it day by day."

Knelt in the midnight cave
   The shepherds and sages three.
   Theirs (do we envy ?) to *see*
The Bread which the Father gave.[3]

---

[1] The literal signification of Bethlehem.
[2] St. John vi. 33, 51, 52.   [3] Ibid. v. 32.

We in the Faith's broad day
  Kneeling—nor once, but at will—
  Take of that Bread our fill,
None "sent empty away."

How should *we* envy *them ?*
  Yet as the grace, the shame,
  If but in boast we claim
The goodlier Bethlehem.

1871.

What tho' we cannot, with the star-led kings,
    Adore the swaddled Babe of Bethlehem,
Behold how sweetly Benediction brings
    A new Epiphany denied to them.
The Mary Mystical 'tis ours to see
    Still from His crib the little Jesus take,
And show Him to us on her altar-knee,
    And sing to Him to bless us for her sake.
Shall we the while be kneeling giftless there?
    In loving faith a richer gold shall please;
A costlier incense in the humblest prayer;
    Nor less the myrrh of penitence than these.
And there between us holy priesthood stands,
Our own Saint Joseph, with the chosen hands.

   1871

TO SAINT JOSEPH.

ON THE DAY OF MY FIRST MASS.

TYPE of the priesthood with its Virgin Spouse,
   The Immaculate Church, our Mother ever fair!
Since even to me God's wondrous grace allows
   An office more than Seraphim may share,
   I kneel to thee, most gentle Saint, and dare
To choose thee patron of the trust.   O make
   My evermore fidelity thy care,
And keep me MARY'S—for Her own sweet sake!
Her knight before, and poet, now Her priest
   (Nor less Her slave:[1] a thousandfold the more),
I glory in a bondage but increased,
   And kiss the chain Her dear De Montfort wore,
   With "Omnia Per Mariam" mottoed o'er,
Which seals me Her apostle—tho' the least.

FEAST OF THE SEVEN DOLORS, March 31, 1871.

[1] The Ven. Grignon De Montfort called his devotion the
"*Slavery* of Jesus in Mary," and himself the "slave, or bonds-
man, of Mary for Jesus."

REPOSING in His altar-home—
　Imprison'd there for love of me—
My Spouse awaits me; and I come
　To visit Him awhile, and be
A solace to his loneliness—
If aught in me can make it less.

But is He lonely? Bend not here
　Adoring angels, as on high?
Ah yes: but yet, when we appear,
　A softer glory floods His eye.
'Tis earth's frail child He longs to see;
And thus He is alone—for me

His Heart, how piningly it aches
　With love unheeded, love despised!
O happy soul, that comes and takes
　The gift as something to be prized:

The lavish'd graces it receives
From that full breast its prayer relieves!

Then, best of lovers, I'll draw near
   Each day to minister relief.
For tho' the thought of year on year
   Of sin should make me die of grief,
Yet day by day my God I see
"Sick and in prison"—all for me!
1866.

HYMN. [1]

Not ours to ask Thee " What is truth?"
   For here it shines the light of light :
And all may see it, age or youth,
   Who will but leave the outer night.
'Tis ours to tread, not seek, the way
That brightens to the perfect day. [2]

[1] Written to be sung at the meetings of a " Christian Doctrine Society" under the patronage of S. Paul.
   Prov. iv. 18.

But this we ask Thee, dearest Lord :
  Let faith, so precious, feed and grow;
And make our lives the more accord
  With fear and love, the more we know;
For thus, too, shall we point the way
That brightens to the perfect day.

Nor have we learnt it save to teach:
  It is for others we are wise:
The humblest has a charge to preach
  Thy kingdom in a nation's eyes :
A nation groping for the way
That brightens to the perfect day.

O thou, our Patron, great Saint Paul,
  Apostle of the West! to thee
We boldly come, and fondly call,
  As children at a father's knee :
Come thou, and with us lead the **way**
That brightens to the perfect **day**!

"*EGO DORMIO, ET COR MEUM VIGILAT.*"[1]

HEART of hearts, a love is thine
    Madly[2] tender, blindly true!
Love in vastness so divine,
    In excess so human too!
Seems it more a burning grief—
Pining, aching for relief.

Seems thou dost not, canst not live,
    Save to sue us for thy rest:
While the all that we can give
    Is as nothing at the best.
Wondrous Lover! shall I say
Thou hast thrown thyself away?

---

[1] " I sleep, and my Heart watcheth."—Cant. v. 2.

[2] " I say, my Jesus, Thou art *mad* with love! I say so, and shall a'ways say so."—S. Mary Magdalen of Pazzi.

Drench'd with anguish—steep'd in woe—
    Thou must needs, insatiate still,
Linger wearily below,
    Prison'd to thy creatures' will:
While the current of the days
Murmurs insult more than praise!

Here I find thee, hour by hour,
    Waiting in thy altar-home,
Full of mercy, full of power—
    Mutely waiting till we come:
Waiting for a soul to bless—
Some poor sinner to caress.

Forth, then, from the fragrant hush,
    Where I almost hear Thee beat,
Bid a benediction gush—
    O'er me, thro' me, thrilling sweet!
Heart of Jesus, full of me,
Fill mine—till it break with Thee!

THE STATIONS OF THE CROSS.

I.

'Tis thou, my cruel heart, but thou
Hast wrought the doom thou weepest now.
'Tis thou hast shouted " Let Him die ! "—
Thy every sin a " Crucify ! "
" I die," He murmurs, " die for thee :
Then sin no more : live true for Me."

II.

Why choose a death of fierce delay
To agonize Thy life away ?
And why do Thy embraces greet
The cross as if Thou deem'st it sweet ?
Thou dost ! A sateless love, we know,
Must ever glut itself on woe.

75

III.

Thou fallest—all too weak! The might
That bears creation's infinite
As tho' its myriad worlds were none,
Has sunk beneath the sins of one!
Ye ruthless stones, thou heedless sod,
How can ye wound your prostrate God?

IV.

They raise Him up, and goad Him on;
When lo, the Mother meets the Son!
How heart rends heart, as eye to eye
Darts the mute anguish of reply!
Sweet Lady, traitor tho' I be,
Yet let me follow Him with thee!

V.

The soldiers fear to see Him die
Too soon for cross and Calvary;

And the Cyrenian, captive made,
Reluctant lends his timely aid.
O happy Simon, didst thou know!
Give me the load thou scornest so!

VI.

Who calls that face unlovely now,
For furrowed cheek and thorn-pierced brow?
To me it never seemed so fair;
For when was love so written there?
Kind Veronica, get me grace
To keep, like thee, that pictured face![1]

VII.

Again He falls! again they deal
Their ruffian blows—those hearts of steel!
He hails His Mother; and the throng
Slink back, to let her pass along.

[1] Our Lord loft the impression of His face on S. Veronica's cloth. This relic of the Passion is still preserved in Rome.

She kneels to soothe Him and caress,
And rage grows dumb at Her distress.

VIII.

The tender women mourn His fate,
With Mary's grief compassionate.
How blest such mourners, He has said:
They shall indeed be comforted.
And He, in turn, has tears for them—
Daughters of lost Jerusalem.

IX.

And yet another fall! Ah why?
'Tis my repeated perfidy.
O Jesus, I but live in vain
If only to be false again!
O Mary, grant me, I implore,
To die this hour, or sin no more!

X.

The Way, the lingering Way is past,
And Calvary's top is gained at last.
With gall the soldiers mock His thirst,
Then strip Him, in their glee accurst.
Descend, ye Angels! round Him flame,
And with your pinions veil His shame!

XI.

Ah see, they stretch Him on the wood:
The blunt nails spurt the Precious Blood!
Nor His alone their every sting;
For Mary hears the hammers ring.
Lord, let that sound my music be
When the death-hour shall strike for me!

XII.

A horror wraps the earth and sky
While three long times go darkly by.

And now, " 'Tis finished!" Jesus cries:
And awfully the God-Man dies.
My heart, canst thou survive content?
Behold, the very rocks are rent!

XIII.

Desolate Mother, clasping there
Thy lifeless Son, yet hear my prayer!
Tho' never was a grief like thine,
And never was a guilt like mine,
Still should I not be dear to thee
When He thou lovest died for me?

XIV.

His lovers lay Him in the tomb,
And leave Him to its peaceful gloom.
Thou sleepest, Lord, Thy labor done;
For me—for all—redemption won:
And I, in turn, as dead would be,
And buried to all else but Thee.

LENT, 1870.

THE PASSION.

WAS ever tale of love like this?
    The wooing of the Spouse of Blood:
Who came to wed us to His bliss
    In those eternal years with God.

Those griefless years, those wantless years,
    He left them—counting loss for gain—
To taste the luxury of tears,
    And revel in the wine of pain!

'Twas sin had mixt the cup of woe
    From Adam pass'd to every lip;
And none could shirk its brimming flow—
    For some a draught, for all a sip:

When Jesus came, athirst to save;
    Nor sucked content a sinless breast;
But grasped the fatal cup, and gave
    That Mother half, then drained the rest.

Enough the milk without the wine.
    When first the new-born Infant smiled,
'Twas merit infinite, divine,
    To cleanse a thousand worlds defiled.

But *we* must take of both. And how
    Could love look on, nor rush to share?
Or hear us moan: " Death's darkness now:
    And Thou, at least, wast never there "?

And so He drank our Marah dry:
    Then filled the cup with wine of heaven.
Who would not live—with Him to die?
    Or not have sinned [1]—when so forgiven?

LENT, 1872.

---

[1] This, of course, is in the sense of the Church's "O felix culpa! O certe necessarium peccatum!"

TO SAINT MARY MAGDALEN.

'MID the white spouses of the Sacred Heart,
   After its Queen, the nearest, dearest thou:
   Yet the auréola around thy brow
Is not the virgins'—thine a throne apart.
Nor yet, my Saint, does faith illumined art
   Thy hand with palm of martyrdom endow:
   And when thy hair is all it will allow
Of glory to thy head, we do not start.
O more than virgin in thy penitent love!
   And more than martyr in thy passionate woe!
     Who knelt not with thee on the gory sod,
How should they now sit throned with thee
     above?
   Or where the crown our worship could bestow
     Like that long gold which wiped the feet of
     God?

1872.

My Magdalen, my own dear Saint,
  Could I but weep my past away
  Like thee at Jesus' feet, the day
He cleansed thy bosom of its taint !

It is not, Sister, that I doubt
  Forgiveness.   He is all too sweet.
  Had I too bathed and kissed His feet,
And heard Him say 'twas blotted out,

I scarce were more assur'd than now :
  For grace on grace has bid me cease
  From fearfulness, and "go in peace,"
With youth renewed in heart and brow.

----

[1] "Who will make my head water, and mine eyes a fountain
of tears?"—Jer. ix. 1.

Yet, by that fire of deathless love,
　Which, kindled at His glance and word,
　Consumed thee for thy Saviour Lord,
As burn the Seraphim above:

By all His tenderness, and those
　Divinely-human looks and ways:
　The thrilling sweetness of His praise,
The joy of mutual repose:

By all the darkness and the scorn
　Of those three hours beneath His cross:
　By all thy share in Mary's loss,
And, happier, in her Easter morn:

Get me the precious gift of tears,
　To flow perennial as thine!
　Thy prayer, dear Saint, shall make them
　　mine,
And wreathe with gems my rescued years.

THE FEAST OF THE FIVE WOUNDS.

DEAR Wounds, it is not mine to see you bleed,
  As Magdalen saw you. Where He reigns above,
You shine in glory. Yet, in very deed,
Remain, as then, five rosy mouths—to plead
  With Him for mercy, and with me for love.

"Behold, upon my Hands I have graven thee!" [1]
  Yea, Lord; on Thy feet, and on Thy Heart.
Thou canst not look on them and not see me.
In all thy woes—from dark Gethsemane
  To Calvary's spear—I bore my cruel part.

Sweet Wounds! Ah, home me! Hide me ever-
      more
  From sin and self. I ask to live and die
Hidden in you. For there is all my store
Of wisdom as of merit. Other lore
  Than that you teach shall pass unheeded by.
1876.

[1] Is. xlix. 16.

My Thorn-crown'd King, thy diadem
   Outshines the bard's, the hero's, wreath.
The tangled gold, the ruby gem,
   How fair they glitter underneath!

And ah, those gems! They flow—they fall!
   The dust receives them! Shall they lie
Unheeded there? O no! They call
   'Adoring legions from the sky.

Yet not for Angels do they flow :
   For sinful men. "And one is mine,
Dear Lord—my very own?" . . . But lo!
   His eyes reproach me: "All are thine."

1875.

Jesus, my King, I have crucified Thee:
Now it is Thy turn to crucify me.
Make Thou the cross—be it only like Thine:
Mix Thou the gall—so Thy love be the wine.

Shrink not to strip me—of all but Thy grace.
Stretch me out well, till I fit in Thy place.
Here are my hands (felon hands!) and my feet:
Drive home the nails, Lord: the pain shall be
    sweet.

Raise me, and take me not down till I die.
Only let Mary, my mercy, stand by.
Last, let the spear while I live do its part :—
Right thro' the heart, my King—right thro' the
    heart!

SACERDOS ALTER CHRISTUS. [1]

THE priest, "another Christ" is he,
  And plights the Church his marriage vows :
Thenceforth in every soul to see
  A daughter, sister, spouse.

Then let him wear the triple cord
  Of father's, brother's, husband's care :
In this partaking with His Lord
  What Angels cannot share.

O sweet new love ! O strong new wine !
  O taste of Pentecostal fire !
Inebriate me, draught divine,
  With Calvary's desire !

[1] S. Bernard.

"I thirst!" He cried. The dregs were drained:
   But still "I thirst!" His dying cry.
While one ungarner'd soul remained,
   The cup too soon was dry.

And shall not *I* be crucified—
   What tho' the fiends, when all is done,
Make darkness round me, and deride
   That not a soul is won?

God reaps from very loss a gain;
   And darkness here is light above.
Nor ever did and died in vain
   Who did and died for love.

" Sufficit discipulo, ut sit sicut
Magister ejus." [1]

THE Priest must bear the Master's cross
　　Of all men most, and take his part
In hours of failure and of loss
　　Like those which wrung the Sacred Heart.

Yet, doubly sure, are others given,
　　Of such sweet comfort, it is worth
The rest to know them : as, in heaven,
　　A moment compensates for earth.

---

[1] " It is enough for the disciple that he be as his Master."—
S. Matt. x. 25.

A LESSON.

I FEEL so helpless, Lady, for the good
   Thou settest me to do: so slight and faint,
All for not standing where I might have stood
   By this time—on the pathway of the saint.

How we forget that we are not our own!
   Not ours the right to throw an hour away:
No, nor a moment: nor to let alone
   One good work offer'd in a crowded day.

For God may want the merit of a deed,
   To grant a grace, or turn a mercy's scale:
And when to *us* this honor comes decreed,
   What shall we answer if His purpose fail?

For this, then, thou dost set me what demands
   A saint? I thank thee. Yet I dare assign
One other cause. So weak *my* lifted hands,
   I the more passive instrument in *thine*.

ANOTHER.

With a pang like the pang of despair
    For one who will soon be dead—
Soon lost to the vain, vain prayer
    Of a heart that has ached and bled—
I turn'd from the foot of the stair
    They were calmly ascending, and fled—
Ay, fled—to the blessèd May air
    And the evening peace o'erhead.

And methought, as I gazed at the West
    Yet aglow in its sunset pride,
"How narrow this grief, this unrest!
    Yon heavens look scornfully wide.
Why rack any longer my breast
    For a conquest to angels denied?
And must not the Good—yea, the Best—
    Still triumph, whatever betide?"

But here something came from the skies:
 'Twas the voice of one near tho' unseen:
And I felt the reproach of those eyes
 Bending o'er me their tender serene.
"For myself was I chasing the prize?
 Or for Her—as a knight for his Queen?
And if *She* tired of wills that despise,
 Where should *I*, pardon'd rebel, have been?"

TO SAINT MATTHIAS.

Dear Saint, thy feast reminds me that to-day,
    Nine years ago, I knelt to Mother Rome,
    To be taken to her bosom—the true home
Found late, yet timely (nor in vain, I pray).
Chosen, perchance (if 'tis not rash to say—
    If ever undeserv'd such graces come)—
    Chosen, like thee, to fill the place of some
Ingrate who had thrown his childhood's faith
    away:
Nay, called to share the Apostolic gift
    Of priesthood with thyself: I boldly claim
Thee patron. Deign be with me when I lift
    My hands to bless, my voice to guide or blame:
Nor let the old enemy, who thought to sift[1]
    The Twelve as wheat, bring me to Judas'
    shame.

1875.

[1] S. Luke xxii. 31.

" 'Tis not the feast that changes with the ever-
    changing times,
  But these that lightly vote away the glories
    of the past —
The joys that dreamlike haunt me with the
    merry matin chimes
  I loved so in my boyhood, and shall dote on
    to the last.

" There still is much of laughter, and a measure
    of old cheer :
  The ivy wreaths, if scanty, are as verdant as
    of yore :
And still the same kind greeting for the uni-
    versal ear :
  But, to me, for all their wishing, 'tis a
    ' merry ' feast no more ! "

I said : and came an answer from the stars to
    which I sighed—
Those stars that lit the vigil of the favored
    shepherd band.
And 'twas as if again the heavens opened deep
    and wide,
    And the carol of the angel-choir new-flooded
    all the land.—

"Good tidings still we bring to all who still
    have ears to hear;
To all who love His coming—the elect that
    cannot ceaso :
And louder rings our anthem to these watchers,
    year by year,
Its earnest of the perfect joy—the everlast-
    ing peace.

" Art thou, then, of these watchers, if thou canst
    not read the sign?
The world was at its darkest when the
    blessed Day-Star shone :

Again 'tis blacker to Her beam : and thou
    must needs repine,
And sicken so near sunrise for the moon
    light that is gone!"

1874.

Saint of the Childhood and the Hidden Life,
　Why is it that thy month is always Lent?
　What hadst thou with the Passion? Mary
　　　went
To Calvary with Jesus; but the knife
Of that fierce sorrow was spared thee. Thy
　　　strife.
　In anxious care and fostering patience spent:
　Now to a stable, now to Egypt sent,
And then long years with humblest labor rife.
But this thy portion of the coming Cross—
　Which o'er thy path its forward shadow threw.
　And is not ours like thine—to walk content
In that long shadow, counting all things loss
　Save what for Jesus we endure or do?—
　To teach us *this* thy month is always Lent.

· March, 1875.

'To find, this greatest day of all the year,
  Our Lady's Mass and Office set aside!   ·

  My day of days—when Holy Church, my bride,
Gave me her hand ; her Angel[1] in mine ear
Announcing words of thrilling joy and fear—
    " Thou art a priest for ever " :—to be de-
      nied.' . . . .
But, suddenly, my Queen herself replied
(I stood at the altar,[2] and 'twas sweet to hear) :
" The words 'tis thine to utter—making bread
  The Body of thy Lord, and wine His Blood—
    What do they but effect the wondrous end
Of mine[3] this day to Gabriel's ' Ave ' said ?
  Behold His wish to be His dear ones' Food
    On thy voice now, as then on mine, depend! "
MARCH 25, 1875.

[1] The bishop (Apoc. cap. 2).
[2] The Holiday remaining, and therefore several Masses having to be said, I had the consolation of thus commemorating my
anniversary.
[3] ' Ecce ancilla Domini," etc.

"THOU ART GONE UP ON HIGH." [1]

"Gone up"! But whither? To a star?
　　Some orb that seems a point of light,
Or one too infinitely far
　　For our fond gaze beneath the night?

Some fairer world, to which our own,
　　With all its vastness, is a grain?
Is 't there the God-Man sets his throne—
　　Fit centre of a boundless reign?

Let science coldly sweep away
　　A fancied Eden here and there
From out the starry space, and say
　　'Tis *all* brute matter—crude and bare:

Or stern philosophy demand
　　"May not yon myriad orbs we ken

---

[1] Ascendisti in altum.—Ps. lxvii.

Be but a pinch of golden sand
    To stretch the narrow minds of men?"—

Yet faith makes answer, meekly bold:
    "Narrow to me your widest lore—
Without the blessèd truth I hold
    That God is Man for evermore.

"He came to wed our life to His:
    As Man was born, and died, and rose:
And in his victor Flesh it is
    Our hopes of Paradise repose.

"He wore it thro' the sweet delay
    That kept Him with His dear ones yet;
Nor put it from him on the day
    He pass'd from topmost Olivet.

"Then still He wears it in the skies—
    Matter in space. And when the cloud
Receiv'd him from the gazers' eyes—
    Before their brimming hearts allowed

"That they had lost Him—swift as thought,
   He reach'd the bright elysian home
His own primeval word had wrought,
   New Eden for the race to come."

1875.

Saint of my birth-day. Then I needs must
    think
  Thou hadst a share in winning me to Rome.
  Perhaps, when furthest from my only home
I had wander'd—none but poison'd wells to
    drink,
The path to truth long lost, and prayer's last
    link
  With God just snapping—thou didst suddenly
    come
  To the rescue: and I knew not, as I clomb
Back o'er the rocks fair-sloping to the brink?
But no. 'Twas She, my blessed Queen and thine,
  The Mother of mercy came—and came alone.
Yet, did She not, my Saint, to thee assign
  Some special care in concert with her own?
To help Her lead me to the light divine,
  And raise me to the sacerdotal throne?

NOT YET.

METHOUGHT the "King of Terrors" came my
    way :
  Whom all men flee, and none esteem it base.
But lo, his smile forbidding me dismay,
    I stood—and dared to look him in the face.
"So soon!" the only murmur in my heart :
  For I had planned the deeds of many years:
Ambitioning atonement, and, in part,
    To reap in joy what I had sown in tears.[1]
Then turning to Our Lady : "O my Queen,
  'Twere very sweet already to have won
My crown, and pass to see as I am seen,
  And nevermore offend thy blessed Son :
Yet would I stay—and for myself, I own :—
To win a little nearer to thy throne."

[1] Ps. cxxv. 5, 6.

OCCASIONAL.

107

DIES VIII. DECEMBRIS.[1]

A.D. MDCCCLXIX.

I.

THERE came an hour, and words[2] were utter'd
    then
  That live to-day and echo evermore.
ONE spoke them to a knot of simple men,
    Who simply took the simple sense they bore:
A promise—such as never tongue or pen
    Of sage oracular had made before;
And a design no *wisdom* could have plann'd,
Save His Who holds the nations in His Hand.

II.

Had less than God so spoken, he had been
  The wildest of all dreamers. What! to make

---

[1] The day on which the Council of the Vatican opened.
[2] St. Matt. xvi. 18.

A poor rude fisher—who had never seen
  A gloom upon his Galilean lake
But fear'd the menace of its boding mien—
  A rock no surge should fret, no tempest
    shake:
The baffled ages foaming at its feet
The broken malice of their ceaseless beat!

III.

God saith, and who shall gainsay? Devils
  first;
  Then fools, their ready dupes. To these, for-
    sooth,
Has seem'd it ever degradation's worst,
  To own the gentle majesty of truth;
Since came the Church to free a world ac-
  curst,
  And heal its heart-ache, and renew its
    youth:
A spring to thaw the universal frost—
Fire-dower'd from her natal Pentecost.

IV.

Error must needs inerrancy defy
   That will not cede its dear delusions breath
(For how should truth be "liberal" to a lie,
   Nor offer God an honorable death ?):
And so along the ages rolls a cry—
   The din of onset at the gates of faith :
'Tis Arius now, now Luther, heads the fray ;
Or bristles up the hydra of to-day.

V.

And patient Rome sits victor over all:
   Her strength in seeming feebleness increased.
She smiles to hear "the storm against the
      wall" [1]
   And lavish'd names of "harlot" and of
      beast,"
And prophets raving of her speedy fall:
   While Satan counts his losses with at least
Tho joy that such solidity of rock
Draws none the fewer to the fatal shock.

[1] Is. xxv. 4.

VI.

Press on, close in, ye gallant ranks of hell!
  Concéntrating the might ye think to bow.
· Stood ever Holy Church, do records tell,
    More one, more conscious, more herself, than
      now?
The Chair of Peter when belov'd so well?
    Or when a Pontiff of serener brow?
He calls: earth hears: her utmost realms resound:
And lo, a thousand mitres gird him round!

VII.

And they who trembled, and had been content
  To scorn with quiet mirth a voice so weak,
Are forced, they find, to yield their panic vent.
    "Another Trent!" rings out the indignant
      shriek:
"This nineteenth century, another Trent!"
    'Tis not so sweet to have the Master speak
When passion, weary of His peaceful sway,
No longer deems it freedom to obey.

VIII.

But speak He will—the blessed words of life.
  How welcome to the soul that thirsts to *know*,
Or views alarm'd the too successful strife
    Of earth with heaven—truth's ebb and error's
      flow.
We murmur thro' our tears, " Decay is rife!
  The sound, the old, the sacred—all will go!"
Fond fear! Whatever faithless thrones expect,
Christ's kingdom stands : He garners His elect.

IX.

The Serpent writhes—his last convulsions these—
  Beneath the foot that tramples his crush'd
    head.
O Lady, worker of thy Son's decrees!
  Thy Rome, thy Pius, trust thee. Deign to
    shed
Thy gracious light, lone star of troubled seas!
  At whose sweet ray the ancient darkness fled.

The Serpent writhes beneath thee. Deign to
    show
He is indeed the Woman's vanquish'd foe.

X.

This day we hail thy victory, and claim
    Thy prayer omnipotent. Nor let it rise
For us alone, that boast to love thy name:
    But those, unhappy, that have dar'd despise.
Who came for them, not less by *thee* He came:
    Thro' *thee* must break unclouded to their eyes.
Ah, Mother's Heart! How long, then, wilt thou
      wait
Till *all* thy children sing "IMMACULATE"?

AUNT MARY.

The shock of loss is less to manhood's years:
    The river of life draws smoother to the deep:
But wherefore *now* this dearth of wonted tears?
    I mourn a mother—yet I cannot weep!

Her love was all a mother's to my youth,
    And stronger seem'd for lack of nature's tie:
Was ever faith as sorely tried, in sooth,
    And proved as true, where duty stood not by?

She grew an image of a growing thought:
    Of that Ideal Mother whom my heart
Kept shaping—ever surer, as it wrought,
    That such must be : thus realized in part.

Her very name, too, led me like a star
    On thro' the twilight to the perfect day:
A note of home's lost music, borne afar
    To stolen child unconsciously astray.

But when the day had broaden'd, the star paled,
  And softly set, its gentle office o'er.
Yet not with this its modest beauty failed:
  To memory's eye it shines for evermore.

I mourn a mother, yet I cannot weep—
  Too peaceful in her peace. Of tributes best.
And what if still she bide in purging keep,
  Nor taste so soon the beatific rest?

Yet peace is with her: sin for ever gone:
  Secure, and hourly nearer, her reward:
And happy prayer, not tears, shall hasten on
  The nobly won fruition of her Lord.

My loss is gain. Another faithful friend,
  A hope, a strength, an advocate, is given,
To watch my course and help me to the end:
  One link the less with earth, the more with
    heaven.

1870.

MUSIC.

When the heart is overflowing,
  Now with sorrow, now with joy;
And its fulness mocks our showing,
  Like a spell that words destroy:

When the soul is all devotion,
  Till its rapture grows a pain,
And to free the pent emotion
  Even prayer's wings spread in vain:

Then but one relief is given:
  Not a voice of mortal birth,
But a language born in heaven,
  And in mercy lent to earth:

Lent to consecrate our sighing,
  Shed a glory on our tears,
And uplift us without dying
  To the Vision-circled spheres.

TO NATURE.

NATURE, to me thy face has ever been
  Familiar as a mother's; yet it grows
  But younger with the wearing years, and
    shows
Fresher—unlike all others I have seen.

The "beings of the mind," though "not of
    clay "—
  "Essentially immortal,"[1] and "a joy
  For ever"[2]—even these may pall and cloy,
For all that poets gloriously say.

Yea, and thy own charms, Nature, when por-
    trayed
  By hand of man, become the spoil of time.
  The seasons mar, not change them: in sub-
    lime
Repose they reign—but evermore to fade.

[1] "The beings of the mind are not of clay :
  Essentially immortal," etc.—Byron.
[2] " A thing of beauty is a joy for ever."—Keats

Whence comes, then, thy perennial youth re-
    newed?
  Thy freshness, as of everlasting morn?
  God's breath is on thee. Of it thou wast
    born,
And with its fragrance is thy life bedewed.

Nor can I need aught sterner than thy face
  To wean me from the things that pass away.
  Not by autumnal lesson of decay,
Or vernal hymn of renovating grace;

But by this fragrance of the Infinite:
  For here my soul catches her native air;
  And tastes the ever fresh, the ever fair,
That wait her in the Gardens of Delight.

TO WORDSWORTH.

GREAT poet, I have tasted and admired
   These many years, but known thee only now—
   With nine-and-twenty winters on my brow,
And much beside that oft thy page inspired.
I find in thee a freshness long desired :
   And take thy song as migrant bird a lake,
   Which first she shunn'd, yet could not all for-
       sake,
Till, last, she nests there—never to be tired.
To nature I have ever turn'd with love,
   But now more fondly, from the world of men.
   'Twas erst for sympathy : with Byron then :
But now, with thee, religiously—to prove
The sweets of contemplation, and emove
   In other minds high thought and holy ken.

I know not which to love the more:
  The morning with its liquid light;
Or evening, with its tender lore
  Of silver lake and purple height.

To morn I say, "The fairer thou:
  For when thy beauties melt away,
'Tis but to breathe on heart and brow
  The gladness of the perfect day."

And o'er the water falls a hue
  That cannot sate a poet's eye:
As though Our Lady's mantle threw
  Its shadow there—and not the sky.

But when has glared the torrid noon,
  And afternoon is gasping low,
The sunset brings a sweeter boon
  Than ever graced the orient's glow.

And I: " As old wine unto new,
　　Art thou to morn, belovèd eve!
And what if dies thy every hue
　　In blankest night ?   We may not grieve.

" Thy fading lulls us as we dote.
　　Nor always blank the genial night :
For when the moon is well afloat,
　　Thou mellowest into amber light."

Is each, then, fairer in its turn ?
　　'Tis hence the music.   Not for me
To wish a dayless morn, or yearn
　　For nightless eve—if these could be.

But give me both—the new, the old :
　　And let my spirit sip the wine
From silver now, and now from gold :
　　'Tis wine alike—alike divine.

SUGGESTED BY A CASCADE.

I.

Not idly could I watch this torrent fall
  Hour after hour: not vainly day by day
  Visit the spot to meditate and pray.
The charm that holds me in its giant thrall
Has too much of the Infinite to pall.
  For tho', like time, the waters pass away,
  They fling a freshness, a baptismal spray,
Which breathes of the Eternal Fount of all.
And so, my God, does Thy revealèd Word—
  In living dogma, or on sacred page—
Flow to us ever new; tho' read and heard
  Immutably the same from age to age.
  And thither Nature sends us to assuage
The higher longings by her voices stirred.

II.

Those voices, like the one I listen here—
  Tho' blending evermore, as tone with tone—
  Are each a perfect music: each, alone,
A faultless melody even to the ear;
But to the heart a mystery as dear
  As the unutter'd meanings of its own.
  And other sweet monotonies, unknown
To all but Catholic hearts, sound year by year,
And day by day, yet weary not. The song
  Of Holy Church, her Mass, her Vespers, flow,
Like this clear stream, unchangingly along;
  Nor newer seem'd a thousand years ago.
  Then where the proof great Nature's self can
    show,
Of source Divine, more exquisitely strong?

    LAKE GEORGE, 1875.

AN EARNEST.

THE world is ever to the child
The same as when on me it smiled
And thrill'd a bosom undefiled:

Its freshness evermore renewed
With sunny morn, and flowers bedewed,
And light-wing'd joys to be pursued.

Then Spring was all, and darling May;
And thro' the Summer's sweet delay
The Golden Age regained its sway:

While Autumn came with thankless pace,
And yielded with a sullen grace
To Winter's hard relentless face.

A change: and these had welcome grown,
As friends of calmer, deeper tone,
Whose thoughts anticipate our own:

While those mov'd dreamlike in the vast,
With vanish'd hopes too bright to last
And memories of a purer past.

I said : " When I have done with earth,
Will that first joy seem nothing worth,
Or know a second, larger, birth ? "

I ween the answer tarried long :
But when it came 'twas clear and strong,
Tho' softer than a linnet's song :

The voice of Faith, forbidding doubt ;
The voice of Nature round about ;
The voice of God—within, without.

" Your conscious heart has told you sooth,
That you regain'd, in gaining Truth,
A freshness better than of youth.

" What need you, then, of hint or view,
More than this foretaste of the dew
That falls where God ' makes all things new' ? "

TO A LADY:

HER death is as of one I knew.
　　Nor only that a friend's distress
　　Is mine. Your sister, could I less
Than picture her another *you?*

She led, you say, an angel's life
　　Ere ever the dividing vows
　　Had wed her to the Virgins' Spouse
And seal'd her for the higher strife.

A chosen soul, then, from her birth;
　　Predestined to the perfect flower:
　　First gather'd for the convent-bower,
Now for a garden not of earth.

You know it, lady ; and the sense
   Forbids the natural tear to flow,
   Unless a joy be with its woe
To give it thankful eloquence.

      •

Nor have you lost her. Veil'd before,
   And cloister'd in a distant home,
   She now is free again to come
And linger near you evermore :

And shield you in a thousand ways,
   And guide your path, and plead your
      cause :
   For so the beatific laws
Of heaven work their Maker's praise.

And this I wish you, dearest friend:
   To catch her mantle with its fold
   Of fragrance and its clasp of gold,
And wear it to as sweet an end.

1869.

TO THE SAME.

My wish is granted. You have caught
   Your sister's mantle, as I prayed :
   Nor any friend is happier made
Than he who weaves this tribute thought.

This Mary takes " the better part " ;
   And walks secure in her retreat,
   Where softly falls about her feet
The shadow of the Sacred Heart :

A shadow and a sunshine too—
   A light, a fragrance, and a rest:
   A peace like that which keeps the blest,
And " inly kisses thro' and thro'."

Ah, joy! The Heart that loves her best
   Is hers—for ever hers. The Spouse
   She chooses for her maiden vows
The truest is and worthiest.

And since her hand in thine was given,
  Sweet Mother, whisper to thy Son
  To set the jewel He has won
Luminous in His crown in heaven.

1870.

VEILED.[1]

Dileotus meus mihi, et ego Illi.—Cant. ii. 16.

No bridegroom mine of change and death:
  My orange-flowers shall never fade.
Immortal dews shall gem the wreath
  When crowns of earth have all decayed.

No bride am I that plights her troth
  With touch of doubt, or trust too fond;
And risks the present, wisely loath
  To search too far the veil'd beyond.

[1] Written, at the same lady's request, for the occasion of her taking the veil.

To me 'tis but the past is veiled—
 The world that mocks with joys that fleet;.
The "Egypt" that so long has failed
 To make its " troubled waters "' sweet:

The world with all its sins and cares,
 Its sorrows gained and graces lost;
The garden of a thousand snares,
 The barren field of blight and frost.

But shines the future clear as truth :—
 A few swift years of prayer and peace,.
Where hearts may know perennial youth,.
 And virtues evermore increase :

And then my Lord, my only love,
 Shall come, and lift the veil, and say :
" Arise, all fair, my spouse, my dove!
 The rain is over—haste, away!

•' Jer. ii. 18.

"'The rain is o'er, the winter gone,[1]
    That sun and summer seem'd to thee.
If sweet the toilsome journey done,
    How sweeter now thy rest shall be!"
    APRIL, 1871,

DEVOTA.[1]

I.

SWEET image of the One I love,
    To whom your infant years were given
(And still the faithful colors[2] prove
    A constancy not all in heaven):

To me a violet near a brink,
    Far-hidden from the beaten way,
And where but rarest flowerets drink
    A freshness from the ripples' play:

[1] Cant. ii. 10, 11.
[2] A child of ten years and dedicated to the Blessed Virgin.
[3] Children thus dedicated have to wear white and blue for a specified time

A lily in a vale of rest,
  And where the angels know a nook
But one shy form has ever prest—
  A poet with a poet's book.

But poet's book has never said
  What I, O lily, find in you:
'Twas never writ and never read,
  Though always old and always new.

And ah, that you must change and go—
  The violet fade, the lily die!
Let others joy to watch you grow;
  Let others smile: so will not I.

Yet smile I should. Is heaven a dream?
  In sooth he needs to be forgiven
Who matches with the things that seem
  A deathless flower, that blooms for heaven.

And while he mourns the onward years
  That sweep you from the things that seem,

Let faith make sunshine on his tears:—
    'Tis heaven is real, and earth the dream.

II.

You little madonna, so very demure!
        You draw me, yet awe me:
        As warning, half scorning,
That kissing a face so religiously pure
Is almost a sacrilege, I may be sure.

Yet, awed as I am, I but love you the more.
        You meet me and greet me
        Serenely and queenly;
And image so sweetly the one I adore
When She was a child in the ages of yore.

Her name it is Mary Regina—your own.
        You share it and wear it
        As flower its dower
Of fragrance—predestined hereafter, full-blown,
To reign with the lilies that circle Her throne.

Be fragrant for me, then, O lily! and pray—
    Each hour, little flower,
    Exhaling availing
Petitions—to Mary the Queen of your May,
To breathe on my Autumn your freshness to-day.

A MEMORY.

I LITTLE took her for a wife.
    She seem'd to stand, with maiden grace,
    Half eager, half averse, to face
The stern realities of life.

But when her tale of bitter wrong
    Had pierced me (tho' her words were few),
    I read her as myself, and knew
How old the heart with such a song.

And yet not quench'd its vital youth,
  Or blighted with a hopeless doom.
  "A flower," I said, "reserv'd to bloom
In sunshine of the future truth.

"She droops, nigh broken, in the night—
  So burthen'd with the rain of woe:
  But each big drop gives purer glow,
And gems her for the dawning light."

A SOUTHERN FLOWER.

A FLOWER of the pale, sad South,
  Nor pale nor sad is she:
  For she blooms on a wonderful tree
That knows not blight or drouth—
  A certain miraculous tree
Our Lady has planted down South.

A rose let me call you, dear girl:
.   A fadeless and thornless rose.
So richly your modesty shows
Its blushes bejewell'd with pearl—
And a dew-drop of grace every pearl—
   That I think of the Mystical Rose.

Then the Lord of the sweet and the fair
   (For Whom is all beauty alone),
I pray Him that floweret so rare
   No hand may dare cull but His own:
That no other bosom may wear
   This rose of the South than His own.

TO MY SISTER.

Our friends who talk of fifty years ago
  All tell us 'tis as yesterday to them:
When you and I were nothingness, we know,
  Save possible buds within a possible stem.
Come fifty more, then, sweet; and let us bloom
  In Paradise together—fadeless flowers:
How brief the yesterday beyond the tomb
    Will then appear—long years but fleeting
      hours!
But cycle upon cycle shall have past,
  And that to-morrow will be still to-day.
So may we well be patient, if, at last,
  Our checker'd April end in endless May:
When that fair future, now so dreamlike seem-
    ing,
Shall make this rueful present seem the dream-
    ing.

TO ———.[1]

"A GARDEN enclosed"[2]—inviolable bound—
  Where may not rest the wafted poison-seed;
But lily and violet deck the virgin ground,
    That knows nor lurking thorn, nor painted
      weed.
  Such, favor'd child, I deem you: you who read
Discoursing lips as tho' they gave you sound,
  Yet hear not 'mid a throng whate'er the greed
Of vanity or malice babble round.
Then who can pity you, or wish you healed,
  Because you miss the melodies of earth?
Nor rather envy you a soul grace-scaled
    To all that blends with these and mars their
      worth:
Seal'd for those others yet to be revealed—
  The heritage of your baptismal birth?

---

[1] A young lady stone-deaf from childhood, but able,
through having learnt the new sign-language, to understand
what is said by watching the speaker's mouth.
[2] Cant. iv. 2.

I.

One friendship more. A truer friend .
I have not known, nor ask to know.
But what the gain, if all must end?
    Where none may reap, 'tis waste to sow.

'Twere better nevermore to meet
    A kindred nature, mind and heart,
If doom'd to murmur "Sad as sweet!
    We found to lose, we met to part."

And stern religion—hear her say
    "Beware, my child, how creatures please:
Refuse to things that pass away
    A love not meant for such as these."

"That pass away." But heart and mind
    Shall never, never pass away:
Nor Holy Church be so unkind
    As call *these* creatures of a day.

'Tis rather hers to bid us weave
  A chain of purer, nobler love,
That lifts our thoughts, from all we leave,
  To faith's sure heritage above.

A love that holds the lov'd one dear
  As God's belov'd, and *so* its own:
And ever with a tender fear
  But lives the more for God alone.

II.

To me the world is less and less
  For each new soul that chimes with mine:
For here 'tis only half *possess*,
  But wholly in the life divine.

To know each other thro' and thro',
  And knowing love, and loving live
All mutual—till we lose and rue :—
  This the rare utmost earth can give.

But when in Beatific Sight
　We wed with Deity, shall blend
Our natures then as light with light—
　The medium God, and God the end:

And know His knowledge, love His love—
　No self to mar the music there:
Approving as His eyes approve,
　And loving as He finds us fair.

Then, with each other sharing Him,
　With Him each other, we possess
In *His* possessing.　Earth is dim
　To this, and wanes to less and less.

This *is* possession: this endures.
　Nor less, but more, the Sum divine:
To me the more that He is yours,
　To you the more that He is mine.

www.ingramcontent.com/pod-product-compliance
Lightning Source LLC
Chambersburg PA
CBHW030603270326
41927CB00007B/1029